Get pupils' knowledge in order with CGP!

Looking for a simple way to help pupils learn all the key facts and methods for Year 6 Maths? Well, look no further — this Knowledge Organiser is the perfect solution!

We've condensed each topic down to the essentials, so it covers exactly what pupils need, with clear diagrams and tables.

And that's not all! There's a matching Year 6 Maths Knowledge Retriever — a great way of making sure pupils have got to grips with the content of every page.

CGP – still the best! ☺

Our sole aim here at CGP is to produce the highest quality books — carefully written, immaculately presented and dangerously close to being funny.

Then we work our socks off to get them out to you — at the cheapest possible prices.

Published by CGP

Editors: Sarah George, Ruth Greenhalgh, Rachel Hickman, Sean McParland, Ali Palin, Sarah Pattison and Dave Ryan.

With thanks to Alison Griffin and Simon Little for the proofreading.

With thanks to Jan Greenway for the copyright research.

ISBN: 978 1 78908 870 0

Printed by Elanders Ltd, Newcastle upon Tyne.
Clipart from Corel®

Based on the classic CGP style created by Richard Parsons.

Contents

Number Basics

Place Value

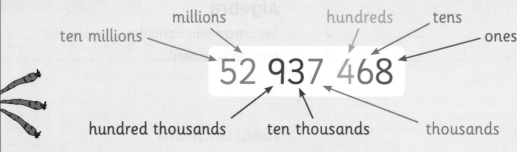

millions
hundreds
tens
ten millions
ones

52 937 468

hundred thousands
ten thousands
thousands

In words, this number is fifty-two million, nine hundred and thirty-seven thousand, four hundred and sixty-eight.

You can use place value to partition:

52 937 468 = 50 000 000 + 2 000 000
+ 900 000 + 30 000
+ 7000 + 400 + 60 + 8

Comparing

The sign < means less than.

The sign > means greater than.

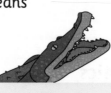

EXAMPLE

Use < or > to compare 3 182 034 and 3 270 967.

3 182 034

Both have 3 millions.

1 is smaller than 2.

3 270 967

So 3 182 034 < 3 270 967.

Ordering

To put whole numbers in order:

1. Look at the number of digits — numbers with more digits are bigger.

2. In numbers with the same number of digits, compare the first digits.

3. If these are the same, keep moving right until the digits are different.

Rounding

Look at the **decider** — the digit to the right of the place being rounded to.

Decider less than 5?	Decider greater than or equal to 5?
Round down	**Round up**

To round to the nearest...

...**ten**, look at the ones digit. ⟶ 481 540

...**hundred**, look at the tens digit. ⟶ 481 500

...**thousand**, look at the hundreds digit. ⟶ 482 000

So 481 537 rounds to:

EXAMPLE

What is 14 526 075 rounded to the nearest ten thousand?

Decider is 6, so round up.

The answer is 14 530 000.

Ascending: from smallest to biggest.
Descending: from biggest to smallest.

EXAMPLE

Put 2 376 226, 919 423, 1 594 038 and 2 381 702 in descending order.

This has no millions, so it's the smallest.

1 594 038 ⟵ This only has 1 million, so it's smaller than the other two.

2 376 226 ⟵

2 381 702 ⟵ Compare the ten thousands.

So the order is 2 381 702, 2 376 226, 1 594 038, 919 423.

Negative Numbers

Adding and Subtracting

Use number lines to add or subtract negative numbers.

To add, start at the negative number and count **on**.

EXAMPLE

Work out −9 + 13.

Sketch a number line.

Start at −9.

Count on 13 places.

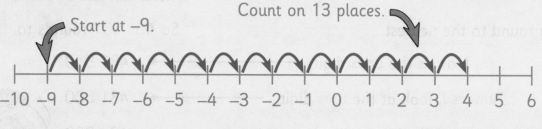

−10 −9 −8 −7 −6 −5 −4 −3 −2 −1 0 1 2 3 4 5 6

So −9 + 13 = 4.

Real-Life Problems

In real-life problems with negative numbers,

you'll often have to find the difference between two numbers.

A 'change' is just the **difference** between the numbers at the start and end.

EXAMPLE

The temperature at midnight was −21 °C. It was −5 °C at noon.
Find the change in temperature.

−21 −11 −5

Count on 1 ten and 6 ones.

So the change is 10 + 6 = 16 °C.

To subtract, count **back**.

What is −2 − 4?

Start at −2.

Count back 4 places.

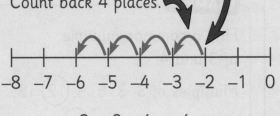

−8 −7 −6 −5 −4 −3 −2 −1 0

So −2 − 4 = −6.

If you have to cross zero, count the places **to** and **after zero**, then add them together.

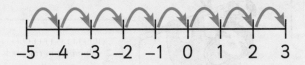

−5 −4 −3 −2 −1 0 1 2 3

There are 5 places from −5 to 0 and 3 places from 0 to 3, so the difference between −5 and 3 is 5 + 3 = 8.

A bank account has −£84 in it. £100 is added. How much is in it now?

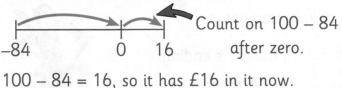

−84   0 16

Count on 100 − 84 after zero.

100 − 84 = 16, so it has £16 in it now.

Finding Differences

To work out differences between negative numbers:

1 Sketch a number line.

2 Count the places between the two numbers.

Find the difference between −36 and −12.

Count on 2 tens and 4 ones.

−36   −16 −12

The difference is 20 + 4 = 24.

A negative temperature is just a temperature **below 0 °C**.

A negative bank balance means you **owe money** to the bank.

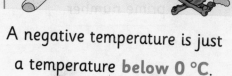

Working with Numbers

Common Factors

Factor	A whole number that divides into the number exactly.
Common factor	A number that is a factor of two or more numbers.

EXAMPLE

Find a common factor of 18 and 21.

Factors of 18: 1, 2, ③, 6, 9 and 18

Factors of 21: 1, ③, 7 and 21

3 is a common factor of 18 and 21.

Common Multiples

Common multiple: a number that is a multiple of two or more numbers.

EXAMPLE

Find a common multiple of 3 and 4.

Multiples of 3: 3, 6, 9, ⑫, 15...

Multiples of 4: 4, 8, ⑫, 16...

12 is a common multiple of 3 and 4.

Numbers in coloured squares are the prime numbers up to 100.

Prime Numbers

A prime number has exactly two factors: **1** and **itself**.

1 1 is NOT a prime number.

2 All prime numbers end in 1, 3, 7 or 9. 2 and 5 are the only exceptions.

3 2 is the only even prime.

(But not all numbers ending in 1, 3, 7 or 9 are prime.)

BODMAS

BODMAS tells you the order to do things in a calculation.

B — Brackets **M** — Multiplication
O —   **A** — Addition
D — Division **S** — Subtraction

EXAMPLE

What is 4 + 10 ÷ 2?

Divide first: 10 ÷ 2 = 5

Then add: 4 + 5 = 9

EXAMPLE

What is (5 − 1) × 3?

Do the brackets first: 5 − 1 = 4

Then multiply: 4 × 3 = 12

Mental Maths

Partition numbers to make it easier to add or subtract.

EXAMPLE

What is 7157 + 816?

816 = 800 + 10 + 6

Add each bit separately:

7157 + 800 = 7957

7957 + 10 = 7967

7967 + 6 = 7973

Work things out in steps.

EXAMPLE

Aleena has 30 marbles. She loses a fifth of them, then buys 4 more. How many does she have now?

1 Work out one fifth of 30:

30 ÷ 5 = 6

2 Subtract from 30:

30 − 6 = 24

3 Add 4: 24 + 4 = 28

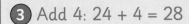
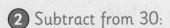
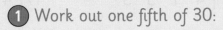

1	2	3	4	5	6	7	8	9	10
11	12	13	14	15	16	17	18	19	20
21	22	23	24	25	26	27	28	29	30
31	32	33	34	35	36	37	38	39	40
41	42	43	44	45	46	47	48	49	50
51	52	53	54	55	56	57	58	59	60
61	62	63	64	65	66	67	68	69	70
71	72	73	74	75	76	77	78	79	80
81	82	83	84	85	86	87	88	89	90
91	92	93	94	95	96	97	98	99	100

Multiplying and Dividing

Long Multiplication

Partition the 2-digit number. **Multiply** each bit separately, then **add**.

EXAMPLE

Work out 1571 × 24.

1 Find 1571 × 4.

4 × 70 = 280, so put 8 in the tens column and carry 2 to the hundreds column.

4 × 1000 = 4000, plus carried 2000 is 6000.

2 Find 1571 × 20.

Don't forget — it's 20 × 1, not 2 × 1.

20 × 70 = 1400, so put 4 in the hundreds column and carry 1 to the thousands column.

20 × 500 = 10 000, plus carried 1000 is 11 000.

Short Division

EXAMPLE

What is 4133 ÷ 17?

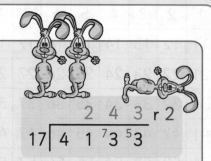

```
      2
17 | 4 1 ⁷3 3
```
17 × 2 = 34, so 17 goes into 41 twice with 7 left over.

```
      2 4
17 | 4 1 ⁷3 ⁵3
```
17 × 4 = 68, so 17 goes into 73 four times with 5 left over.

```
      2 4 3 r 2
17 | 4 1 ⁷3 ⁵3
```
17 × 3 = 51, so 17 goes into 53 three times with 2 left over.

So 4133 ÷ 17 = 243 remainder 2

Long Division

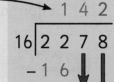

EXAMPLE

Work out **2278 ÷ 16**.

16 goes into 22 once, so write 1 above 22. 22 − 16 = 6,

so write 6 below and move the next digit (7) down.

```
        1 4 2
16 2 2 7 8
   -1 6
        6 7
      - 6 4
          3 8
        - 3 2
            6
```

16 × 4 = 64, so 16 goes into 67 four times. Write 4 above the 7. 67 − 64 = 3, so write 3 below and move the next digit down.

16 × 2 = 32, so 16 goes into 38 twice. Write 2 above the 8.

38 − 32 = 6, so write 6 below.

There are no more digits to bring down, so this is the remainder.

So 2278 ÷ 16 = 142 remainder 6

3 Add together.

```
    1 5 7 1
  ×     2 4
    6 2 8 4   ① ←①
+ 3 1 4 2 0   ② ←②
  3 7 7 0 4
          1
```

1571 × 24 = 6284 + 31 420

= 37 704

Remainders

Remainder: the bit left over after a division.

Write a remainder:

as a number	as a fraction	as a decimal
27 ÷ 5 = 5 r 2	27 ÷ 5 = $5\frac{2}{5}$	27 ÷ 5 = 5.4

EXAMPLE

A tray can hold 8 mugs. How many trays are needed to hold 52 mugs?

52 ÷ 8 = 6 remainder 4

6 trays won't be enough, so 7 trays will be needed.

Calculation Problems

Wordy Problems

1   Pick out the important information in the question.

2   Turn it into maths.

EXAMPLE

Romesh has 16 red blocks, 18 yellow blocks and 9 blue blocks. How many blocks does he have in total?

16 + 18 = 34. Then add on the 9: 34 + 9 = 43.

So he has 43 blocks in total.

Estimating

To estimate answers by rounding:

1   Round to easier numbers — e.g. to the nearest ten or the nearest whole number.

2   Work out the calculation using the easier numbers.

EXAMPLE

Estimate $119 \div 9$.

Round both numbers to the nearest ten:

$119 \div 9 \approx 120 \div 10 = 12$

$\approx$ means "approximately equal to".

EXAMPLE

Estimate 10.84×6.12.

Round both numbers to the nearest whole number:

$10.84 \times 6.12 \approx 11 \times 6 = 66$

Solve problems with more than one calculation
by working things out one step at a time.

EXAMPLE

A drink is made from 2000 ml
of lemonade and 400 ml of
orange juice. Jenny shares the
drink equally between 12 glasses.
How many ml is in each glass?

2000 ml + 400 ml = 2400 ml

It is shared between 12 glasses,

so work out 2400 ÷ 12.

24 ÷ 12 = 2, so 2400 ÷ 12 = 200.

So there is 200 ml in each glass.

EXAMPLE

Cinema tickets cost £8 for adults
and £4.50 for children. Sally buys
3 adult tickets and 2 child tickets.
How much change does she get
from £40?

3 adult tickets costs 3 × £8 = £24

2 child tickets costs 2 × £4.50 = £9

Sally spends £24 + £9 = £33 in total,

so she gets £40 − £33 = £7 change.

Checking

Estimate to check answers.

Either find two numbers the answer
lies between, or round and check that
your answer is close to the estimate.

EXAMPLE

Use estimation to check 6.1 × 8.1 = 49.41.

6.1 × 8.1 ≈ 6 × 8 = 48. This is close
to 49.41, so the answer seems sensible.

EXAMPLE

Use estimation to check
6.74 × 9 = 52.62.

6 × 9 = 54 and 7 × 9 = 63

6.74 is between 6 and 7,

so the answer to 6.74 × 9

is between 54 and 63.

So this answer is wrong.

Fraction Basics

Equivalent Fractions

Equivalent fractions have different denominators, but are equal.

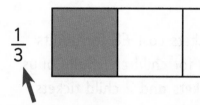

$\frac{1}{3}$

These represent the same amount, so they're equivalent.

$\frac{3}{9}$

Matching Denominators

To put a group of fractions over the same denominator:

1 Find a common multiple of the denominators.

2 Turn each fraction into an equivalent fraction with the common multiple as the denominator.

Simplifying

Simplifying: turning a fraction into an equivalent fraction with the smallest possible numbers.

Divide the top and bottom by the same number.

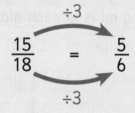

$$\frac{15}{18} \overset{\div 3}{\underset{\div 3}{=}} \frac{5}{6}$$

Dividing by the biggest common factor of the top and bottom will get you straight to a simplified fraction.

> Give answers to fraction questions as simplified fractions.

EXAMPLE

Turn $\frac{3}{4}$ and $\frac{4}{5}$ into equivalent fractions with the same denominator.

Multiples of 4: 4, 8, 12, 16, ⃝20 ..

Multiples of 5: 5, 10, 15, ⃝20 25...

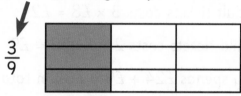

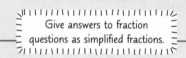

Ordering Fractions

If all fractions have the same denominator, compare the numerators. Fractions with bigger numerators are bigger.

For fractions with different denominators:

> Write them as equivalent fractions with the same denominator.

> Compare the numerators.

Which of $\frac{5}{8}$ and $\frac{7}{12}$ is bigger?

Find equivalent fractions.

$$\begin{array}{cc} \times 3 & \times 2 \\ \frac{5}{8} = \frac{15}{24} & \frac{7}{12} = \frac{14}{24} \\ \times 3 & \times 2 \end{array}$$

$15 > 14$, so $\frac{5}{8}$ is bigger.

Ordering Fractions Bigger Than 1

Turn any mixed numbers into improper fractions. Then follow the steps for proper fractions above.

Put $\frac{11}{6}$, $\frac{12}{5}$ and $2\frac{4}{15}$ in order from biggest to smallest.

1. Turn the mixed number into an improper fraction.

$$2\frac{4}{15} = \frac{(2 \times 15) + 4}{15} = \frac{34}{15}$$

2. Turn into equivalent fractions.

$$\begin{array}{ccc} \times 5 & \times 6 & \times 2 \\ \frac{11}{6} = \frac{55}{30} & \frac{12}{5} = \frac{72}{30} & \frac{34}{15} = \frac{68}{30} \\ \times 5 & \times 6 & \times 2 \end{array}$$

3. Put them in order by comparing numerators. $\dfrac{72}{30}, \dfrac{68}{30}, \dfrac{55}{30}$

4. Write them in their original forms. $\dfrac{12}{5}, 2\dfrac{4}{15}, \dfrac{11}{6}$

Use the common multiple 20:

$$\begin{array}{cc} \times 5 & \times 4 \\ \frac{3}{4} \longrightarrow \frac{15}{20} & \frac{4}{5} \longrightarrow \frac{16}{20} \\ \times 5 & \times 4 \end{array}$$

So the answer is $\dfrac{15}{20}$ and $\dfrac{16}{20}$.

Fraction Calculations

Adding and Subtracting Fractions

You can only add or subtract fractions with the same denominator.

Only add or subtract the numerators
— leave the denominators as they are.

EXAMPLE

Work out $\frac{3}{4} - \frac{1}{9}$.

$$\overset{\times 9}{\underset{\times 9}{\frac{3}{4}}} \longrightarrow \frac{27}{36} \qquad \overset{\times 4}{\underset{\times 4}{\frac{1}{9}}} \longrightarrow \frac{4}{36}$$

$$\frac{27}{36} - \frac{4}{36} = \frac{27-4}{36} = \frac{23}{36}$$

Mixed Numbers

To add or subtract mixed numbers:

1 Convert them into improper fractions.

2 Make sure the improper fractions have the same denominator.

EXAMPLE

Work out $4\frac{2}{3} + 2\frac{2}{3}$.

$$4\frac{2}{3} = \frac{(4 \times 3) + 2}{3} = \frac{14}{3}$$

$$2\frac{2}{3} = \frac{(2 \times 3) + 2}{3} = \frac{8}{3}$$

$$\frac{14}{3} + \frac{8}{3} = \frac{22}{3} = 7\frac{1}{3}$$

Give your answer as a mixed number.

Dividing by Whole Numbers

To divide a fraction by a whole number:

$$\frac{2}{5} \div 3 = \frac{2}{5 \times 3} = \frac{2}{15}$$

Multiply the denominator by the whole number.

Leave the numerator alone.

$$\frac{2}{5} > \frac{2}{15}$$

The denominator gets bigger, so the fraction is smaller.

Multiplying Two Fractions

1 Multiply the numerators.

2 Multiply the denominators.

3 Simplify if needed.

EXAMPLE

Work out $\frac{5}{6} \times \frac{2}{3}$.

1 ÷ 2 **3**

$$\frac{5}{6} \times \frac{2}{3} = \frac{5 \times 2}{6 \times 3} = \frac{10}{18} = \frac{5}{9}$$

2 ÷ 2

Give your answer as a simplified fraction.

When you multiply two proper fractions, the answer is **smaller** than either fraction.

$$\frac{1}{3} \times \frac{1}{5} = \frac{1}{15}$$

$\frac{1}{15} < \frac{1}{3}$

$\frac{1}{15} < \frac{1}{5}$

Dividing by 4 is the same as multiplying by $\frac{1}{4}$.

This is because multiplying and dividing are inverses.

EXAMPLE

$\frac{3}{8}$ of a bottle of squash is shared equally between 5 people. What fraction of the bottle do they each get?

$$\frac{3}{8} \div 5 = \frac{3}{8 \times 5} = \frac{3}{40} \text{ of the bottle}$$

$$\frac{3}{7} \div 4 = \frac{3}{7 \times 4} = \frac{3}{28}$$

$$\frac{3}{7} \times \frac{1}{4} = \frac{3 \times 1}{7 \times 4} = \frac{3}{28}$$

Decimals

Multiplying and Dividing by 10, 100 and 1000

To multiply by: **Shift all of the digits:**

10 $\Longrightarrow$ 1 place to the left

100 $\Longrightarrow$ 2 places to the left

1000 $\Longrightarrow$ 3 places to the left

O t h   TO t
$8.53 \times 10 = 85.3$

O t h   HTO
$8.53 \times 100 = 853$

O t h   ThHTO
$8.53 \times 1000 = 8530$

Add zeros as placeholders to fill any empty places.

Multiplying Decimals

1 Do a multiplication using whole numbers.

2 Work out how many times bigger this answer is than the answer to the decimal multiplication.

3 Divide to find the answer to the decimal multiplication.

EXAMPLE

Work out 3.18×6.

Find 318×6.

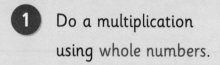

$$
\begin{array}{r}
3\ 1\ 8 \\
\times \qquad 6 \\
\hline
1\ 9\ 0\ 8 \\
{\scriptstyle 1\ \ 4}
\end{array}
$$

This is 100 times bigger than 3.18×6.

$1908 \div 100 = 19.08$

So $3.18 \times 6 = 19.08$

Dividing Decimals

Do a division with whole numbers.

$\Downarrow$

Work out how much bigger this is than the answer to the decimal division.

$\Downarrow$

Divide to find the answer to the decimal division.

Estimate to check your answer.

To **divide by 10**, shift the digits **1 place** to the right.

$$29.43 \div 10 = 2.943$$

To **divide by 100**, shift the digits **2 places** to the right.

$$1350 \div 100 = 13.50 = 13.5$$

Remove any unneeded zeros.

To **divide by 1000**, shift the digits **3 places** to the right.

$$41 \div 1000 = 0.041$$

Rounding Decimals

1 Count the number of decimal places you need to keep.

2 Look at the decider (the next digit to the right).

3 Round up if the decider is 5 or bigger. Round down if the decider is 4 or smaller.

EXAMPLE

Work out 3.72 ÷ 4.

Find $372 \div 4$.

$$4 \overline{\smash{)}3\ 7\ {}^{1}2} = 9\ 3$$

So $372 \div 4 = 93$

$93 \div 100 = 0.93$

So $3.72 \div 4 = 0.93$

$3.72 \div 4 \approx 4 \div 4 = 1$

EXAMPLE

Round 6.492 to 2 decimal places.

You need to keep 2 decimal places, so the decider is the thousandths digit.

$$6.49|2$$

2 is smaller than 5, so round down to 6.49

EXAMPLE

Round 14.97 to 1 decimal place.

$$14.9|7$$ The decider is bigger than 5, so round up to 15.0

Your answer must have 1 decimal place.

Fractions, Decimals & Percentages

Using Equivalent Fractions

You can use equivalent fractions to write some fractions as decimals.

This works if there's an equivalent with a denominator of 10, 100 or 1000.

$$\frac{1}{10} = 0.1$$

$$\frac{24}{30} = \frac{8}{10} = 0.8 \qquad (\div 3)$$

$$\frac{1}{100} = 0.01$$

$$\frac{7}{25} = \frac{28}{100} = 0.28 \qquad (\times 4)$$

$$\frac{1}{1000} = 0.001$$

$$\frac{11}{200} = \frac{55}{1000} = 0.055 \qquad (\times 5)$$

Common Conversions

Learn all of these conversions:

$$\frac{1}{4} = 0.25 = 25\%$$

$$\frac{3}{4} = 0.75 = 75\%$$

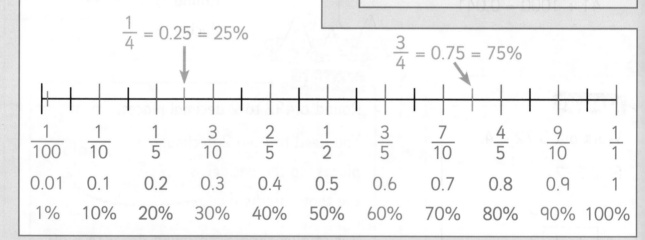

$\frac{1}{100}$	$\frac{1}{10}$	$\frac{1}{5}$	$\frac{3}{10}$	$\frac{2}{5}$	$\frac{1}{2}$	$\frac{3}{5}$	$\frac{7}{10}$	$\frac{4}{5}$	$\frac{9}{10}$	$\frac{1}{1}$
0.01	0.1	0.2	0.3	0.4	0.5	0.6	0.7	0.8	0.9	1
1%	10%	20%	30%	40%	50%	60%	70%	80%	90%	100%

Fractions as Divisions

A fraction is just another way of writing a division.

$$\frac{\text{numerator}}{\text{denominator}} = \text{numerator} \div \text{denominator}$$

So $\frac{1}{5} = 1 \div 5 = 0.2$.

Work out the division to convert a fraction into a decimal.

Converting Between Fractions, Decimals and Percentages

Work out the division (numerator ÷ denominator).

Fraction  **Decimal**

Use a denominator of 10 if there's 1 decimal place,
100 if there are 2 and 1000 if there are 3. Put the digits
after the point as the numerator. Simplify if needed.

Multiply by 100 and add a % sign.

Decimal  **Percentage**

Divide by 100 and remove the % sign.

Put it over a denominator of 100, remove the % sign and simplify if needed.

Percentage **Fraction**

Find an equivalent fraction with a denominator
of 100 and add a % sign to the numerator.

EXAMPLE

Write $\frac{5}{8}$ as a decimal.

$\frac{5}{8} = 5 \div 8$ Work out 5000 ÷ 8 first.

$$\begin{array}{r} 6\ 2\ 5 \\ 8\ \overline{)\ 5\ 0\ ^20\ ^40} \end{array}$$

So 5 ÷ 8 = 625 ÷ 1000 = 0.625

EXAMPLE

What is 0.62 as a fraction?

0.62 has 2 decimal places,
so use a denominator of 100.

$$\overset{\div 2}{\frac{62}{100} = \frac{31}{50}}$$
$$\div 2$$

Relative Sizes

Scaling

Multiply to scale amounts up.

Divide to scale amounts down.

EXAMPLE

4 pencils cost 44p.
How much will 9 pencils cost?

Scale down to find the cost
of 1 pencil: 44p ÷ 4 = 11p

Then scale up to find the cost
of 9 pencils: 11p × 9 = 99p

Ratios

Ratios compare one part
to another part.

There are 4 circles and 2 squares.

For every 2 circles, there is 1 square.

The **ratio** is "2 circles to 1 square".

You can write this ratio as **2 : 1**.

Unequal Sharing

Three steps to share things unequally:

1 Find the total number of shares.

2 Work out what one share is.

3 Multiply to find the number
of shares you want.

Scale Factors

The **scale factor** is the number
each side of a shape is multiplied
by when it is enlarged.

EXAMPLE

Enlarge this shape by
a scale factor of 2.

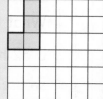

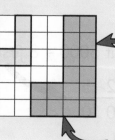

Multiply each side length
by the scale factor.

New lengths = old lengths × 2

New length = 3 × 2 = 6

New length = 2 × 2 = 4

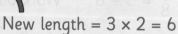

EXAMPLE

A bracelet has 2 red beads for every 7 white beads. There are 6 red beads. How many white beads are there?

×3 (2 red to 7 white) ×3
(6 red to ? white)

7 × 3 = 21 white beads

The ratio of red to white beads is 2:7.

Proportions

Proportions compare one part to the whole.

4 pieces of fruit in every 5 are apples.
$\frac{4}{5}$ of the pieces of fruit are apples.

1 piece of fruit in every 5 is a banana.
$\frac{1}{5}$ of the pieces of fruit are bananas.

EXAMPLE

There are 20 cows in a field.
3 in every 4 cows are brown.
How many of the cows are brown?

There are 20 ÷ 4 = 5 lots of 4 cows in the field.

3 cows in each lot are brown, so 3 × 5 = 15 cows are brown.

EXAMPLE

Matt and Jill share £60.
Matt gets £7 for every £3 Jill gets.
How much does Jill get?

There are 7 + 3 = 10 shares in total.

Each share is £60 ÷ 10 = £6.

Jill gets 3 × £6 = £18.

Matt and Jill share the money in the ratio 7:3.

KEEP OFF THE GRASS

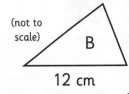

To find a scale factor, divide an enlarged length by the matching original length.

EXAMPLE

Shape B is an enlargement of shape A.
Find the scale factor of the enlargement.

Base of shape B = 12 cm
Base of shape A = 4 cm
Scale factor = 12 ÷ 4 = 3

A
4 cm

(not to scale)

B
12 cm

Using Percentages

Percentages of Amounts

To find 10% of a number, divide it by 10.

To find 50% of a number, divide it by 2.

To find **20%**, find 10% then **multiply by 2**.

To find **5%**, find 10% then **divide by 2**.

EXAMPLE

Find 10% of 720.

10% of 720 = 720 ÷ 10

= 72

EXAMPLE

A bag has 15% off in a sale. It originally cost £60. How much is the discount?

Numbers as Percentages of Other Numbers

To write a number as a percentage of a total:

1 Put the total amount as the denominator of a fraction.

2 Put the number you're looking for as the numerator.

3 Convert to a percentage.

EXAMPLE

There are 8 green fish and 12 yellow fish in a tank.
What percentage of the fish in the tank are green?

1 In total, there are 8 + 12 = 20 fish. $\dfrac{8}{20}$

2 8 fish are green.

3 $\dfrac{8}{20} = \dfrac{40}{100} = 40\%$ are green.

×5 ... ×5

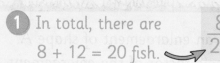

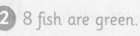

EXAMPLE

Find **30%** of 80.

10% of 80 = 80 ÷ 10 = 8

30% of 80 = 8 × 3 = 24

Compare amounts by converting them into percentages.

EXAMPLE

Ayo won £25 in a prize draw and spent £7 of it. Tanya won £10 and spent £2. Who spent a bigger percentage of their prize money?

Ayo:

×4

$$\frac{7}{25} = \frac{28}{100} = 28\%$$

×4

Tanya:

×10

$$\frac{2}{10} = \frac{20}{100} = 20\%$$

×10

28% > 20%, so Ayo spent a bigger percentage.

10% of £60 = £60 ÷ 10 = £6

5% of £60 = £6 ÷ 2 = £3

So 15% = £6 + £3 = £9

15% off!

EXAMPLE

Niall has 600 ml of slime. He uses 420 ml in a prank. Greta has 500 ml of slime. She uses 300 ml to make a slime monster. Who uses a smaller percentage of their slime?

÷6

Niall: $\frac{420}{600} = \frac{70}{100} = 70\%$

÷6

÷5

Greta: $\frac{300}{500} = \frac{60}{100} = 60\%$

÷5

60% < 70%, so Greta uses a smaller percentage.

Sequences and Formulas

Finding Rules for Sequences

Rule of a sequence:

tells you how to get from one term to the next.

Find the rule by working out the difference between the terms.

EXAMPLE

The first four terms in a sequence are 1, 4, 7 and 10. What is the rule to get from one term to the next?

+3   +3   +3
1   4   7   10

The rule is "add 3 to the previous number".

EXAMPLE

The first four terms in a sequence are 27, 23, 19 and 15. What is the rule to get from one term to the next?

−4   −4   −4
27   23   19   15

The rule is "take away 4 from the previous number".

Continuing a Sequence

Use the rule to find more terms in the sequence.

EXAMPLE

The first four terms in a sequence are 2, 9, 16 and 23. Find the next three terms in the sequence.

+7   +7   +7
2   9   16   23

The rule is "add 7 to the previous number".

Next three terms:

23 + 7 = 30

30 + 7 = 37

37 + 7 = 44

Writing Formulas

EXAMPLE

All the cars in a garage have 4 wheels.

Write a formula to work out the total number of wheels of any number of cars in the garage.

EXAMPLE

The first four terms in a sequence are 13, 11, 9 and 7. Find the next two terms in the sequence.

The rule is "take away 2 from the previous number".

Next two terms: $7 - 2 = 5$

$5 - 2 = 3$

Formula: a rule that connects two or more quantities, so you can work out one quantity when you know the others.

1 Write out the formula.

2 Write it again, but with numbers in place of the words.

3 Work it out in stages.

EXAMPLE

The formula for the cost in £ of a pizza is:
Cost = 5 + number of toppings × 0.5
How much does a pizza with
4 toppings cost?

Cost = 5 + no. of toppings × 0.5

Cost = 5 + 4 × 0.5

Cost = 5 + 2 = 7

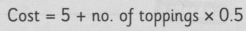 Use BODMAS.

The pizza costs £7.

Total number of wheels
= number of cars × 4

The thing you're trying to find goes before '='.

EXAMPLE

The formula for the area of a triangle is:
Area = $\frac{1}{2}$ × base × height
What is the area of the triangle below?

Area = $\frac{1}{2}$ × base × height

Area = $\frac{1}{2}$ × 6 × 5

Area = $\frac{1}{2}$ × 30 = 15 cm^2

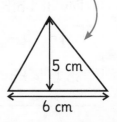

5 cm

6 cm

Missing Numbers

Using Symbols for Missing Numbers

Use a symbol to stand for a number in a problem that you need to find.

1 Choose a symbol and write down what it stands for.

2 Write the information in the question using numbers and symbols.

3 Get the symbol on its own.

Dani multiplies her age by 3. She gets the answer 27. How old is Dani?

◯ = Dani's age

◯ × 3 = 27

Divide both sides by 3:

◯ = 27 ÷ 3 = 9

So Dani is 9.

Lyle says: "If you double the number of sweets I have, then subtract 7, you get 9." How many sweets does he have?

☐ = number of sweets

9 + 7 is double the number of sweets Lyle has.

9 + 7 = 16, so 2 × ☐ = 16.

Divide both sides by 2:

☐ = 16 ÷ 2 = 8

So Lyle has 8 sweets.

Pairs of Missing Numbers

Some problems have two missing numbers.

Try numbers until you find ones that work.

P × Q = 8. Find two possible pairs of values for P and Q.

P = 1: 1 × 8 = 8, so Q = 8.
P = 2: 2 × 4 = 8, so Q = 4.

P = 4 and Q = 2 and P = 8 and Q = 1 are also possible pairs of values.

Using Letters for Missing Numbers

You can also use letters to stand for missing numbers.

If you call the missing number x, then:

x + 3 means "add 3 to the number"

x − 1 means "subtract 1 from the number"

2x means "multiply the number by 2"

$\frac{x}{2}$ means "divide the number by 2"

EXAMPLE

Roz has 28 stamps. Roz has four times as many stamps as Lin. How many does Lin have?

The number Lin has is unknown.

Call this n stamps.

Then Roz has 4 × n stamps.

So 4n = 28

n = 28 ÷ 4 = 7   ← Divide both sides by 4.

So Lin has 7 stamps.

Sometimes you can simplify the question to make it easier to solve.

EXAMPLE

6 + △ + △ + ☆ = 17. Find a possible pair of values for △ and ☆.

1 Simplify the question.

6 + △ + △ + ☆ = 17
6 + 2△ + ☆ = 17
2△ + ☆ = 11

So you need values for △ and ☆ that give 2△ + ☆ = 11.

2 Find numbers that work.

Try △ = 1:

2△ = 2 × 1 = 2
2 + ☆ = 11, so ☆ = 9

Some other pairs of answers are △ = 2 and ☆ = 7 and △ = 4 and ☆ = 3.

Units

Converting Units

Multiply to go from a big unit to a small unit.

Divide to go from a small unit to a big unit.

These are the conversion factors:

Length

1 cm	10 mm
1 m	100 cm
1 km	1000 m

Mass

1 kg	1000 g

Volume

1 litre	1000 ml

Converting Units of Time

You may need to use a few steps to convert units of time.

1 minute	60 seconds
1 hour	60 minutes
1 day	24 hours
1 week	7 days
1 year	365 days

There are 366 days in a leap year.

EXAMPLE

How many hours are in 2 weeks?

1 First convert to days:

1 week = 7 days

2 weeks = 2 × 7 = 14 days

2 Then convert to hours:

1 day = 24 hours

14 days = 14 × 24 = 336 hours

EXAMPLE

How many seconds are in 4 hours?

First convert to minutes:

1 hour = 60 minutes   4 × 60 = 240 minutes

EXAMPLE

A bottle holds 0.5 litres of water. How many ml is this?

1 litre = 1000 ml

So multiply by 1000:

0.5 litres × 1000 = 500 ml

EXAMPLE

How far is 25 miles in kilometres?

1 First divide by 5:

$25 \div 5 = 5$

2 Then multiply by 8:

$5 \times 8 = 40$ km

Miles and Kilometres

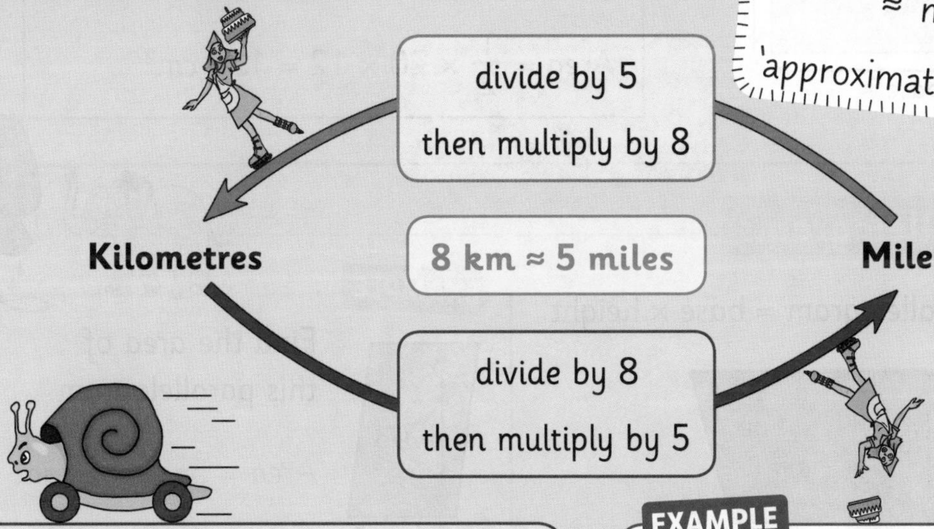

divide by 5

then multiply by 8

Kilometres

8 km ≈ 5 miles

Miles

divide by 8

then multiply by 5

'$\approx$' means 'approximately equal to'.

Then convert to seconds:

1 minute = 60 seconds

240 × 60 = 14 400 seconds

EXAMPLE

How many miles are in 96 km?

1 First divide by 8:

$96 \div 8 = 12$

2 Then multiply by 5:

$12 \times 5 = 60$ miles

Measurement   29

Perimeter, Area and Volume

Area and Perimeter

Area is the space inside a 2D shape.

Perimeter is the distance around the outside of a shape.

Area of Triangles

Area of a triangle $= \frac{1}{2} \times$ base $\times$ height

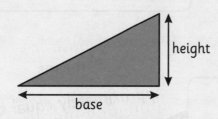

base

height

EXAMPLE

Find the area of this triangle.

12 cm

20 cm

The base is 20 cm.

The height is 12 cm.

Area $= \frac{1}{2} \times 20 \times 12 = 120$ cm^2

Area of Parallelograms

Area of a parallelogram = base × height

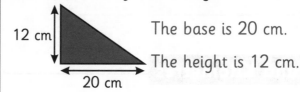

height

base

EXAMPLE

Find the area of this parallelogram.

8 cm

4 cm

Area = base × height

Area $= 4 \times 8 = 32$ cm^2

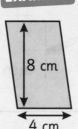

EXAMPLE

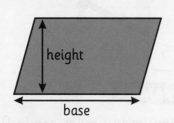

6 cm

9 cm

Find the area of the grey part of this parallelogram.

Area of parallelogram $= 9 \times 6 = 54$ cm^2

Area of coloured triangle $= \frac{1}{2} \times 9 \times 6 = 27$ cm^2

Area of grey part $= 54 - 27 = 27$ cm^2

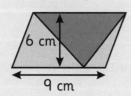

Shapes with the same perimeter can have different areas:

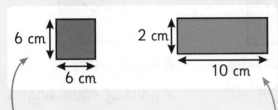

Perimeter = 6 + 6 + 6 + 6 = 24 cm

Area = 6 × 6 = 36 cm²

Perimeter = 2 + 10 + 2 + 10 = 24 cm

Area = 10 × 2 = 20 cm²

Shapes with the same area can have different perimeters.

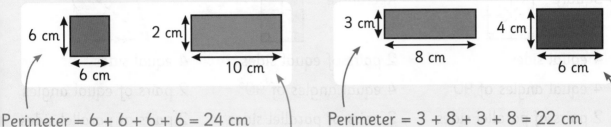

Perimeter = 3 + 8 + 3 + 8 = 22 cm

Area = 8 × 3 = 24 cm²

Perimeter = 4 + 6 + 4 + 6 = 20 cm

Area = 6 × 4 = 24 cm²

Volume of Cubes and Cuboids

Volume: the amount of space a 3D shape takes up.

Volume of a cuboid = length × width × height

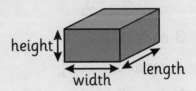

Calculate the volume of this cuboid.

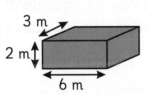

Volume = 3 × 6 × 2

Volume = 36 m³

Volume is measured in 'cubic' units:

m³ →	cubic metres
cm³ →	cubic centimetres
mm³ →	cubic millimetres
km³ →	cubic kilometres

2D Shapes

Quadrilaterals

A **quadrilateral** is a shape with 4 sides.

Square

4 equal sides

4 equal angles of 90°

2 pairs of parallel sides

4 lines of symmetry

Rectangle

4 equal angles of 90°

2 pairs of equal sides

2 pairs of parallel sides

2 lines of symmetry

Rhombus

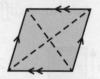

4 equal sides

2 pairs of equal angles

2 pairs of parallel sides

2 lines of symmetry

Other Polygons

Equilateral triangle

3 equal sides

3 equal angles of 60°

No parallel sides

3 lines of symmetry

Isosceles triangle

2 equal sides

2 equal angles

No parallel sides

1 line of symmetry

Regular polygon: a shape with all equal sides and equal angles.

Irregular polygon: a shape that doesn't have all equal sides and equal angles.

Circles

radius: distance from the edge to the centre

diameter: distance across the circle through the centre

circumference: the outside edge of a circle

EXAMPLE

Draw an equilateral triangle with sides of 3 cm.

Equilateral triangles have three equal sides and three 60° angles.

Draw the first side.

Kite

2 pairs of equal sides
1 pair of equal angles
No parallel sides
1 line of symmetry

Parallelogram

2 pairs of equal sides
2 pairs of equal angles
2 pairs of parallel sides
No lines of symmetry

Trapezium

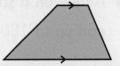

1 pair of parallel sides

Most trapeziums have no lines of symmetry, but ones like this have exactly one:

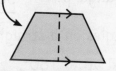

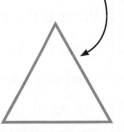

The diameter is twice the radius.

EXAMPLE

The diameter of a circle is 14 cm. What is the radius of the circle?

Diameter = 2 × radius

Radius = diameter ÷ 2

Radius = 14 ÷ 2

= 7 cm

Drawing Polygons

1. Measure and draw sides with a ruler.

2. Measure and draw angles with a protractor.

Then draw the final line to complete the triangle.

Mark the 60° angle with a dot.

Draw a 3 cm line through the dot.

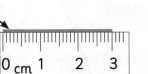

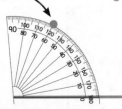

Angles

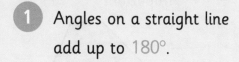

Angle Rules

1 Angles on a straight line add up to 180°.

$$a + b + c = 180°$$

2 Angles around a point add up to 360°.

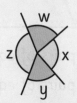

$$w + x + y + z = 360°$$

EXAMPLE

What is the size of angle p?

Angles on a straight line add up to 180°.

So 56° + 71° + p = 180°

p = 180° − 56° − 71° = 53°

EXAMPLE

What is the size of angle q?

Angles around a point add up to 360°.

So 128° + 64° + 90° + q = 360°

q = 360° − 128° − 64° − 90° = 78°

3 Vertically opposite angles are equal.

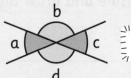

$$a = c \text{ and } b = d$$

EXAMPLE

What is the size of angle r?

r and the 54° angle are vertically opposite, so they are equal. So r = 54°.

Angles in a Triangle

Angles in a triangle add up to 180°.

EXAMPLE

What is the size of angle x in this triangle?

Angles in a Quadrilateral

Angles in a quadrilateral add up to 360°.

EXAMPLE

What is the size of angle s in this quadrilateral?

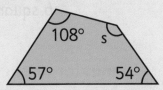

Angles in a quadrilateral add up to 360°, so

s + 54° + 57° + 108° = 360°

s = 360° − 54° − 57° − 108°

$\quad$ = 141°

The triangle is isosceles, so this angle is 67°.

Angles in a triangle add up to 180°, so x + 67° + 67° = 180°.

x = 180° − 67° − 67° = 46°

Angles in Polygons

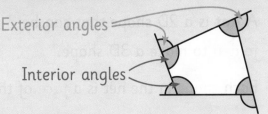

Exterior angles

Interior angles

For all polygons:

Interior angle = 180° − exterior angle

Sum of exterior angles = 360°

Sum of interior angles = (n − 2) × 180°

n is the number of sides.

For regular polygons ONLY:

1 All interior angles are equal.

2 All exterior angles are equal.

3 Exterior angle = $\dfrac{360°}{n}$

EXAMPLE

Find the exterior and interior angles in a regular hexagon.

A hexagon has 6 sides, so n = 6.

Exterior angle = $\dfrac{360°}{n}$

$\qquad\qquad$ = $\dfrac{360°}{6}$ = 60°

Interior angle = 180° − 60°

$\qquad\qquad$ = 120°

3D Shapes

Nets and 3D Shapes

A **net** is a 2D shape that can be folded to make a 3D shape.

Each shape in the net is a face of the 3D shape.

Cube

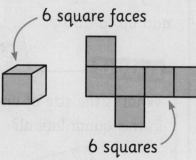

6 square faces

6 squares

More About Nets

A 3D shape can have more than one net.

Triangular prism

> **EXAMPLE**
>
> Draw two different nets for this cube.
>
>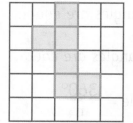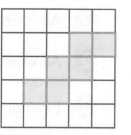

> **EXAMPLE**
>
> Circle the nets that will fold up to make a triangular prism.
>
>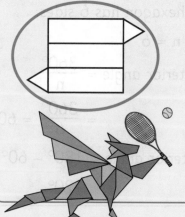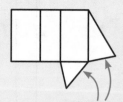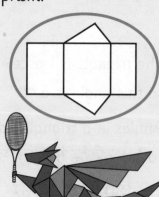
>
> The triangular faces would touch, so it won't make a triangular prism.

Cuboid

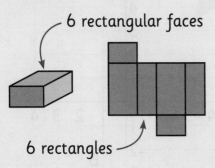

6 rectangular faces

6 rectangles

Square-based pyramid

4 triangular faces

1 square face

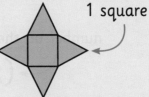

4 triangles

1 square

Tetrahedron (triangle-based pyramid)

4 triangular faces

4 triangles

2 triangular faces

3 rectangular faces

2 triangles

3 rectangles

Drawing 3D Shapes

3D shapes can be drawn on isometric (dotty) paper.

Only draw vertical or diagonal lines on isometric paper — never horizontal lines.

EXAMPLE

Draw the cuboid formed by this net on the isometric paper below.

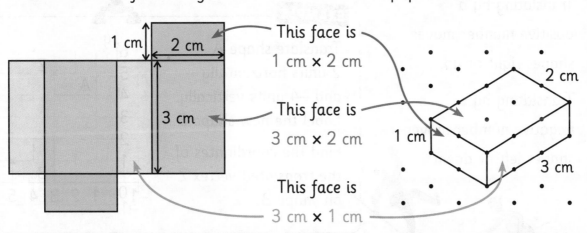

This face is 1 cm × 2 cm

This face is 3 cm × 2 cm

This face is 3 cm × 1 cm

Coordinates & Transformations

Coordinates

Each quarter of the grid is called a quadrant.

Coordinates tell you the position of a point.

number on the horizontal axis

$$(x, y)$$

number on the vertical axis

If x is positive, the point is right of the origin.

If x is negative, the point is left of the origin.

If y is positive, the point is above the origin.

If y is negative, the point is below the origin.

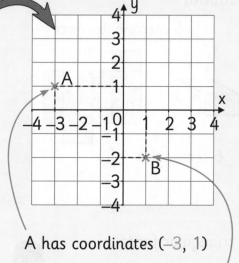

A has coordinates (−3, 1)

B has coordinates (1, −2)

The origin has coordinates (O, O).

Translations

Translation: when a shape slides from one place to another.

woof
meow

Translating by a positive number moves shapes right or up.

Translating by a negative number moves shapes left or down.

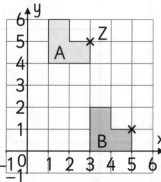

EXAMPLE

Translate shape A 2 units horizontally and −4 units vertically. Label the new shape B.

Find the coordinates of the translated vertex Z on shape B.

Missing Coordinates

Use shape facts to find missing coordinates.

> ### EXAMPLE
>
> The shape on the right is a square.
> What are the coordinates of point A?
>
>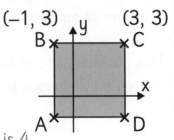
>
> A is directly below B, so they have the same
> x-coordinate. So the x-coordinate of A is −1.
>
> The difference between the x-coordinates of B and C is 4,
> so each side of the square is 4 units. A is 4 units below B,
> so the y-coordinate of A is 3 − 4 = −1. So A has coordinates (−1, −1).

Reflections

Reflect shapes in a mirror line.

Each point and its reflection are the same distance from the mirror line.

Translate the shape
2 units to the right
and 4 units down.

The coordinates
of the translated
vertex Z are (5, 1).

> **1** Count the number of
> units to the mirror line.
>
> **2** Count the same number
> on the other side of
> the mirror line.
>
> **3** Draw the reflected point.
>
>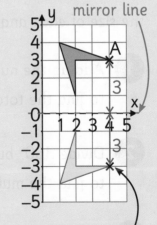
>
> Vertex A is 3 units above the x-axis, so the
> reflected vertex A is 3 units below the x-axis.

Pie Charts

Pie Chart Basics

Pie charts: show things as proportions.

A slice of a pie chart is called a sector.

A bigger sector means a bigger proportion.

This pie chart shows the favourite sports chosen by 24 pupils in a Year 6 class.

This is a quarter of the pie chart, so a quarter of the class chose football.

One quarter of 24 is 6.

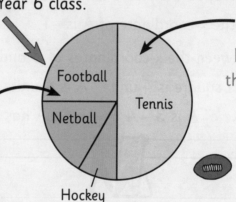

This is half of the pie chart, so half of the class chose tennis.

Half of 24 is 12.

Angles In a Pie Chart

There are 360° in a circle.

Total of the angles in a pie chart = 360°

Drawing Pie Charts

Use a multiplier to work out the size of each angle.

1. Add up the numbers to find the total.

2. Divide 360° by the total to find the multiplier.

3. Multiply each number by the multiplier to get the angle.

EXAMPLE

The table on the right shows the number of different coloured balls in a bag.
Draw a pie chart to show this information.

1. Total = 28 + 51 + 17 + 24 = 120

2. Multiplier = 360 ÷ 120 = 3

3. Red = 28 × 3 = 84°
   Blue = 51 × 3 = 153°
   Green = 17 × 3 = 51°
   Yellow = 24 × 3 = 72°

EXAMPLE

A survey asked people to vote for their favourite vegetable.
This pie chart shows the results. What is the angle for "turnip"?

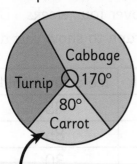

Total of the angles = 360°, so 170° + 80° + ? = 360°.

360° − 170° − 80° = 110°

So the angle for "turnip" = 110°.

80° is the smallest sector,
so "carrot" got the fewest votes.

170° is the biggest sector,
so "cabbage" got the most votes.

Interpreting Pie Charts

Turn angles into numbers
by finding a fraction or
percentage of the pie chart.

EXAMPLE

This pie chart shows
how 60 pupils travelled
to school. How many
pupils walked?

The 'walk' sector is 150°.

Whole chart = 360°,

> Divide the top and
> bottom by 30.

so the fraction is $\frac{150°}{360°} = \frac{5}{12}$.

$\frac{5}{12} \times 60 = 25$ pupils walked.

Colour	Red	Blue	Green	Yellow
Number	28	51	17	24

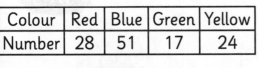

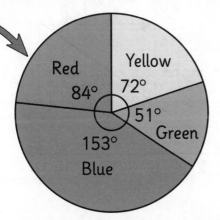

Working with Data

Line Graphs

Line graphs: show how something changes.

To plot points on a line graph:

1 Read up from the horizontal axis and across from the vertical axis.

2 Draw a point where the two lines meet.

3 Repeat for each point, then join them up with straight lines.

EXAMPLE

The table below shows the number of ice creams sold at a shop over four weeks. Draw a line graph to show this data.

Week	Ice creams sold
1	95
2	85
3	30
4	75

Conversion Graphs

Use conversion graphs to convert between different units.

Put one unit on the horizontal axis and one unit on the vertical axis.

EXAMPLE

The graph on the right converts between miles and kilometres.

What is 10 miles in kilometres?

Read up from the horizontal axis:

10 miles = 16 km

What is 24 kilometres in miles?

Read across from the vertical axis:

24 km = 15 miles

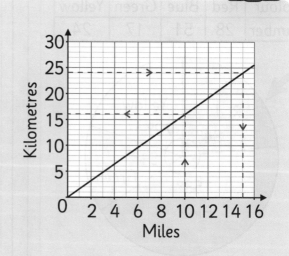

42   Statistics

"Ice creams sold" is on the vertical axis.

Ice creams sold (vertical axis, values: 0, 10, 20, 30, 40, 50, 60, 70, 80, 90, 100)

Week (horizontal axis, values: 1, 2, 3, 4)

The weeks are on the horizontal axis.

EXAMPLE

This line graph shows the temperature in a garden on one day. How much warmer was it at 2 pm than at 11 am?

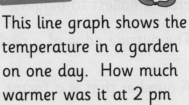

Temperature (°C) (vertical axis: 0, 2, 4, 6, 8, 10, 12, 14, 16, 18, 20, 22)

Time (horizontal axis: 9 am, 12 pm, 3 pm)

Read up from the 'Time' axis.

At 11 am it was 14 °C.

At 2 pm it was 21 °C.

So it was 21 − 14 = 7 °C warmer.

The Mean

The mean is sometimes called 'the average'. To find the mean:

1 Add up all of the numbers.

2 Divide the total by how many numbers there are.

EXAMPLE

Find the mean of these numbers:

5, 6, 11, 7, 4, 9

5 + 6 + 11 + 7 + 4 + 9 = 42

There are 6 numbers.

42 ÷ 6 = 7

So the mean is 7.

EXAMPLE

The weights of some bags of birdseed were 47 g, 53 g, 55 g and 45 g. What was the mean weight?

47 + 53 + 55 + 45 = 200

There are 4 numbers. 200 ÷ 4 = 50

So the mean weight was 50 g.

Glossary

Area	The space inside a 2D shape.
Ascending	From smallest to biggest.
Circumference	The outside edge of a circle.
Common factor	A number that is a factor of two or more numbers.
Common multiple	A number that is a multiple of two or more numbers.
Conversion graph	A graph used to convert between different units.
Descending	From biggest to smallest.
Diameter	The distance across a circle, through the centre.
Equivalent fractions	Fractions that have different denominators, but are equal.
Factor	A whole number that divides into the number exactly.
Formula	A rule that connects two or more quantities, so you can work out one quantity when you know the others.
Irregular polygon	A shape that doesn't have all equal sides and equal angles.
Line graph	A graph with points that are joined by lines, which shows how something changes.
Mean	A kind of average found by adding up all the values then dividing by the total number of values.
Multiple	A number in a times table. E.g. multiples of 6 are 6, 12, 18...

Negative number	A number less than zero.
Net	A 2D shape that can be folded to make a 3D shape.
Perimeter	The distance around the outside of a shape.
Pie chart	A circular chart that shows things as proportions.
Prime number	A number with exactly two factors: 1 and itself.
Proportion	Something that compares one part of an amount to the whole amount.
Quadrilateral	A shape with 4 sides.
Radius	The distance from the edge of a circle to the centre.
Ratio	Something that compares one part of an amount to another part.
Regular polygon	A shape with all equal sides and equal angles.
Remainder	The bit left over after a division.
Scale factor	The number each side of a shape is multiplied by in an enlargement.
Sequence	A list of numbers (or shapes) that follow a pattern. There is a rule that links each term to the one before.
Simplifying	Turning a fraction into an equivalent fraction with the smallest possible numbers.
Term	Each number in a number sequence.
Translation	When a shape slides from one place to another on a grid.
Volume	The amount of space a 3D shape takes up.

Index